## Copyright © 2023 by S. J. Matthews (Author)

This book is protected by copyright law and is intended solely for personal use. Reproduction, distribution, or any other form of use requires the written permission of the author. The information presented in this book is for educational and entertainment purposes only, and while every effort has been made to ensure its accuracy and completeness, no guarantees are made. The author is not providing legal, financial, medical, or professional advice, and readers should consult with a licensed professional before implementing any of the techniques discussed in this book. The content in this book has been sourced from various reliable sources, but readers should exercise their own judgment when using this information. The author is not responsible for any losses, direct or indirect, that may occur from the use of this book, including but not limited to errors, omissions, or inaccuracies.

*We hope this book has been informative and helpful on your journey to understanding and celebrating older adults. Thank you for your interest and support!*

*Title: Advanced Techniques for Detecting and Preventing 51% Attacks on Proof-of-Work Blockchains*
*Subtitle: Advanced Techniques for Defense*

**Series: Defending Bitcoin: A Comprehensive Guide to 51% Attack Prevention**
**By S. J. Matthews**

*"Bitcoin is a remarkable cryptographic achievement and the ability to create something that is not duplicable in the digital world has enormous value."*
Eric Schmidt, Former CEO of Google

*"Bitcoin is a technological tour de force."*
Bill Gates, Co-Founder of Microsoft

*"Bitcoin is the beginning of something great: a currency without a government, something necessary and imperative."*
Nassim Taleb, Author of "The Black Swan"

*"Bitcoin is a remarkable cryptographic achievement... The ability to create something which is not duplicable in the digital world has enormous value."*
Roger Ver, Bitcoin Investor and Entrepreneur

*"Bitcoin is a remarkable cryptographic achievement and the ability to create something that is not duplicable in the digital world has enormous value."*
Peter Thiel, Co-Founder of PayPal

*"Bitcoin is a very exciting development, it might lead to a world currency. I think over the next decade it will grow to become one of the most important ways to pay for things and transfer assets."*
Kim Dotcom, Founder of Megaupload

*"Bitcoin is a protocol that could change the world, like the web did. Don't miss out."*
Andreas Antonopoulos, Bitcoin Educator and Author

*"Bitcoin is better than currency in that you don't have to be physically in the same place and, of course, for large transactions, currency can get pretty inconvenient."*
Bill Gates, Co-Founder of Microsoft

# Table of Contents

**Introduction ......................................................... 8**

*Understanding the need for continued innovation in blockchain security ........................................................... 8*

*An overview of emerging technologies and strategies for blockchain security ............................................................ 12*

*The potential impact of these innovations on the blockchain ecosystem ......................................................... 15*

**Chapter 1: Sharding and Scalability ....................... 17**

*Understanding the concept of sharding and how it can improve blockchain scalability ........................................... 17*

*Examples of blockchain networks that use sharding, such as Ethereum 2.0 ........................................................... 20*

*The potential drawbacks and limitations of sharding .... 22*

**Chapter 2: Cross-Chain Interoperability ............... 24**

*The importance of interoperability between different blockchain networks ....................................................... 24*

*An overview of existing cross-chain solutions, such as atomic swaps and wrapped tokens ................................. 27*

*The potential impact of cross-chain interoperability on the blockchain ecosystem ................................................. 30*

**Chapter 3: Zero-Knowledge Proofs and Privacy .... 32**

*An introduction to zero-knowledge proofs and their role in preserving privacy on the blockchain ......................... 32*

    *Examples of blockchain networks that use zero-knowledge proofs, such as Zcash* ........................ *34*

    *The potential impact of zero-knowledge proofs on the broader technology landscape* ........................ *36*

## Chapter 4: Quantum Computing and Blockchain Security ........................ 39

    *An overview of quantum computing and its potential impact on blockchain security* ........................ *39*

    *Existing efforts to develop quantum-resistant blockchain solutions* ........................ *43*

    *The potential implications of quantum computing for the broader technology landscape* ........................ *46*

## Chapter 5: Decentralized Governance and Security ........................ 50

    *The importance of decentralized governance for ensuring blockchain security* ........................ *50*

    *An overview of existing decentralized governance solutions, such as DAOs* ........................ *53*

    *The potential impact of decentralized governance on the blockchain ecosystem* ........................ *55*

## Chapter 6: Regulatory Compliance and Security ... 58

    *The importance of regulatory compliance for ensuring blockchain security* ........................ *58*

*An overview of existing regulatory frameworks for blockchain technology, such as the FATF guidelines ...... 61*

*The potential impact of regulatory compliance on the broader technology landscape ......................................... 66*

## Chapter 7: Investment and Innovation in Blockchain Security ................................................................. 69

*An overview of investment trends and emerging players in the blockchain security space......................................... 69*

*The potential impact of continued innovation on the blockchain security landscape ......................................... 72*

*Opportunities and challenges for entrepreneurs and investors in the blockchain security space....................... 75*

## Conclusion ....................................................... 78

*Key takeaways from the book ............................................ 78*

*Implications for the future of blockchain security .......... 81*

*Call to action for stakeholders in the blockchain ecosystem ........................................................................ 83*

## Key Terms and Definitions ..................................... 85
## Supporting Materials............................................. 87

# Introduction
## Understanding the need for continued innovation in blockchain security

Blockchain technology has come a long way since the inception of Bitcoin in 2009. Today, blockchain is being used for a variety of applications, from financial transactions to supply chain management and beyond. However, as the use cases for blockchain technology continue to grow, so do the challenges of ensuring its security. One of the most pressing security concerns for blockchain technology is the threat of 51% attacks on proof-of-work blockchains.

A 51% attack occurs when a single entity or group of entities control more than 50% of the computing power in a proof-of-work blockchain network. This gives them the ability to manipulate the blockchain's transaction history and potentially steal funds or cause other disruptions. Although 51% attacks are still relatively rare, they have occurred in the past and could become more common in the future as blockchain technology continues to grow.

To prevent 51% attacks and other security threats, there is a need for continued innovation in blockchain security. This includes the development of new technologies and strategies that can improve the security of blockchain networks, as well as the implementation of best practices for maintaining the security of existing blockchain networks. In this section, we will explore the need for continued innovation in blockchain security and the potential consequences of failing to invest in this area.

The Need for Continued Innovation in Blockchain Security

Blockchain technology is inherently secure due to its decentralized and distributed nature. However, this security can be compromised if a single entity or group of entities gains control over the majority of the network's computing power. This is why proof-of-work blockchains, which rely on computing power to validate transactions and maintain the network, are vulnerable to 51% attacks.

To prevent 51% attacks and other security threats, it is essential to continue investing in blockchain security research and development. This includes the exploration of new technologies and strategies that can improve the security of blockchain networks, as well as the implementation of best practices for maintaining the security of existing blockchain networks.

One area where continued innovation is needed is in the development of new consensus mechanisms that are resistant to 51% attacks. Proof-of-work is just one of several consensus mechanisms used in blockchain technology, and while it has proven to be effective in many cases, it is not immune to attacks. Other consensus mechanisms, such as proof-of-stake and delegated proof-of-stake, offer different levels of security and may be more resistant to 51% attacks.

Another area where continued innovation is needed is in the development of new cryptographic techniques that can improve the privacy and security of blockchain transactions. Zero-knowledge proofs, for example, offer a way to verify the validity of a transaction without revealing any sensitive information about the transaction itself. This can help prevent attacks that attempt to exploit weaknesses in the blockchain's privacy and security features.

Finally, continued innovation is needed in the development of new security standards and best practices for maintaining the security of blockchain networks. This includes the implementation of secure coding practices, regular security audits, and the use of multi-factor authentication and other security measures to prevent unauthorized access to blockchain networks.

The Consequences of Failing to Invest in Blockchain Security

Failing to invest in blockchain security research and development can have serious consequences for the blockchain ecosystem as a whole. In addition to the risk of

51% attacks and other security threats, failing to invest in blockchain security can also lead to a loss of trust in blockchain technology.

Blockchain technology is still in its early stages of development, and many people are still skeptical of its potential. If blockchain networks are seen as being insecure or vulnerable to attacks, this could undermine public confidence in the technology and slow its adoption. This could, in turn,

# An overview of emerging technologies and strategies for blockchain security

Blockchain technology has come a long way since its inception, and its applications are continually expanding. With this expansion, the need for security in the blockchain ecosystem has become increasingly important. This need has led to the development of new emerging technologies and strategies for blockchain security. In this section, we will provide an overview of these emerging technologies and strategies and their potential impact on the blockchain ecosystem.

One of the key emerging technologies for blockchain security is sharding. Sharding is a technique used to improve blockchain scalability by breaking down the blockchain network into smaller, more manageable parts called shards. Each shard is responsible for processing a subset of transactions, reducing the burden on the entire network. This results in faster transaction processing times and reduced costs. Ethereum 2.0, for example, is a blockchain network that uses sharding to improve its scalability.

Another emerging technology for blockchain security is cross-chain interoperability. This technology allows for seamless transactions between different blockchain networks. Currently, blockchain networks operate in isolation, which limits their functionality and usefulness. Cross-chain interoperability enables the transfer of assets and data across different blockchain networks, creating new opportunities for innovation and growth. Some examples of cross-chain solutions include atomic swaps and wrapped tokens.

Zero-knowledge proofs are another emerging technology for blockchain security. These proofs allow for private transactions, where the details of the transaction remain hidden from the public blockchain. This is achieved by proving that a certain statement is true without revealing any additional information. Zero-knowledge proofs are currently being used by blockchain networks such as Zcash, which allows for private transactions on its network.

Quantum computing is an emerging threat to blockchain security. Currently, most blockchains use cryptographic algorithms that are based on the difficulty of solving certain mathematical problems. However, quantum computers have the potential to solve these problems much faster than traditional computers, rendering current cryptographic algorithms obsolete. To address this issue, efforts are underway to develop quantum-resistant cryptographic algorithms and blockchain solutions.

Decentralized governance is an emerging strategy for blockchain security. Decentralized governance enables decision-making on the blockchain network to be decentralized, which makes the network more resilient to attacks and reduces the potential for centralization. DAOs are an example of decentralized governance in action, where decisions are made by the community rather than a central authority.

Regulatory compliance is another emerging strategy for blockchain security. Regulatory compliance ensures that blockchain technology is used in a responsible and legal manner, reducing the potential for illicit activities such as money laundering and terrorism financing. The Financial Action Task Force (FATF) has developed guidelines for regulating blockchain technology, which are being implemented by various countries and organizations.

In summary, emerging technologies and strategies for blockchain security are constantly evolving to address the challenges and threats to the blockchain ecosystem. These technologies and strategies have the potential to transform the way we use and interact with blockchain technology, enabling new opportunities for innovation and growth.

## The potential impact of these innovations on the blockchain ecosystem

The potential impact of emerging technologies and strategies for blockchain security cannot be overstated. These innovations have the potential to transform the blockchain ecosystem in significant ways, providing new solutions to longstanding problems and opening up new opportunities for developers, investors, and users alike.

One of the most significant impacts of these innovations is their potential to increase the scalability and throughput of blockchain networks. Sharding, for example, could allow blockchain networks to process significantly more transactions per second, potentially making them more suitable for mainstream adoption. Cross-chain interoperability could similarly enable the creation of more complex and interconnected blockchain ecosystems, potentially driving increased innovation and investment in the space.

Another key impact of these innovations is their potential to enhance the privacy and security of blockchain networks. Zero-knowledge proofs, for example, could enable the creation of more private and anonymous transactions, potentially making blockchain networks more attractive to a wider range of users. Decentralized governance solutions could similarly enhance the security and resilience of blockchain networks, potentially making them more resistant to attacks and censorship.

At the same time, these innovations are not without their potential drawbacks and limitations. Sharding, for example, could introduce new security risks or vulnerabilities, while quantum computing could potentially render existing blockchain security measures obsolete. It will be important for developers and stakeholders to carefully consider these potential risks and limitations as they work to integrate these emerging technologies and strategies into their blockchain projects.

Overall, the potential impact of emerging technologies and strategies for blockchain security is significant and far-reaching. These innovations have the potential to transform the blockchain ecosystem in ways that we can only begin to imagine, driving increased innovation, investment, and adoption in the space. As we continue to explore these emerging technologies and strategies, it will be important for us to carefully consider their potential impacts and work together to ensure that they are integrated in ways that maximize their potential benefits while minimizing their potential risks.

# Chapter 1: Sharding and Scalability
## Understanding the concept of sharding and how it can improve blockchain scalability

Blockchain technology has emerged as a promising solution for a wide range of applications, from financial transactions to supply chain management and beyond. However, one of the biggest challenges facing blockchain networks today is their limited scalability. Most blockchain networks are limited in the number of transactions they can process per second, making them unsuitable for high-volume use cases.

Sharding is one potential solution to this problem. The concept of sharding is based on the idea of breaking up a larger database into smaller, more manageable pieces. In the context of blockchain networks, sharding involves dividing the network into smaller, more manageable shards or partitions, each of which can process a subset of the total network transactions.

The key benefit of sharding is its potential to significantly increase the scalability of blockchain networks. By dividing the network into smaller, more manageable shards, sharding can increase the total number of transactions that a network can process per second, potentially making it more suitable for high-volume use cases.

At the same time, sharding is not without its potential drawbacks and limitations. One potential issue is the risk of reduced security. When a network is divided into smaller shards, each shard may be more vulnerable to attacks, since there are fewer nodes and resources to protect it. This risk can be mitigated through careful design and implementation, but it is important to consider it when evaluating the potential benefits of sharding.

Another potential issue is the challenge of maintaining consensus across multiple shards. When a network is divided into multiple shards, it becomes more difficult to ensure that all nodes agree on the state of the network. This can be addressed through the use of techniques such as cross-shard communication and atomic cross-shard transactions, but these techniques can add additional complexity and overhead to the network.

Despite these potential challenges, the concept of sharding has generated significant interest and experimentation in the blockchain community. Several prominent blockchain networks, including Ethereum 2.0, are currently exploring sharding as a potential solution to their scalability challenges. As these networks continue to develop and refine their sharding implementations, it will be important to carefully evaluate the potential benefits and drawbacks of this approach, and to explore additional techniques and strategies for improving blockchain scalability.

## Examples of blockchain networks that use sharding, such as Ethereum 2.0

Ethereum is a blockchain network that has been exploring sharding as a means of improving scalability. Ethereum 2.0, also known as Eth2 or Serenity, is the latest version of the Ethereum network and is designed to be more scalable, secure, and sustainable than its predecessors.

In Ethereum 2.0, sharding is a key component of the network's scalability solution. The network is divided into smaller, interconnected pieces called "shards," each of which can process transactions in parallel with the others. This means that the network's capacity to process transactions can be increased by adding more shards to the network.

Ethereum 2.0 uses a Proof-of-Stake (PoS) consensus algorithm instead of the Proof-of-Work (PoW) algorithm used by earlier versions of the network. This is because PoS is more energy-efficient and can support a higher number of transactions. In PoS, validators stake their own Ether to secure the network and are rewarded for doing so. The more Ether a validator stakes, the more likely they are to be selected to create the next block and earn a reward.

The Ethereum 2.0 sharding design allows for different shards to have different validators, enabling more validators to participate in securing the network. This means that the network can handle more transactions and achieve higher throughput, making it more scalable.

Another benefit of sharding is that it can improve the overall security of the network. In a non-sharded network, a single node failure or attack can bring down the entire network. With sharding, the failure or attack is limited to a single shard, which reduces the impact on the rest of the network.

Ethereum 2.0 also includes other features and improvements to further enhance the network's scalability and security, such as the use of stateless clients and the introduction of the Beacon Chain. These features are designed to work in tandem with sharding to create a more robust and efficient network.

Overall, the use of sharding in Ethereum 2.0 is a promising development for the blockchain industry. It has the potential to significantly improve the scalability and security of blockchain networks, enabling them to handle a larger number of transactions and support more complex applications.

## The potential drawbacks and limitations of sharding

While sharding can offer a significant improvement in scalability for blockchain networks, it is not without its limitations and potential drawbacks. In this section, we will explore some of the challenges and limitations associated with sharding.

1. Security Risks: One of the most significant concerns associated with sharding is security risks. In sharded networks, each shard operates independently and has its own set of validators. This can create a situation where a malicious actor could compromise a single shard and gain control over a significant portion of the network's computing power. This could potentially lead to a 51% attack, where the attacker has enough computing power to control the network and manipulate transactions.

2. Data Availability: Another potential drawback of sharding is data availability. In sharded networks, nodes are only required to store data for a specific shard. This means that nodes may not have access to all the data on the network, which can make it difficult to verify transactions and maintain the integrity of the blockchain. This problem can be mitigated by implementing cross-shard communication protocols, but this can add complexity and reduce the efficiency of the network.

3. Difficulty of Implementation: Sharding is a complex technique that requires careful planning and execution. Designing an effective sharding strategy requires a deep understanding of the underlying technology and the needs of the network. Additionally, implementing a sharding strategy can be challenging, as it requires changes to the network's architecture and may require significant changes to the network's software.

4. Interoperability: Sharding can also create interoperability challenges, as different shards may use different consensus mechanisms or have different rules for validating transactions. This can make it difficult for different shards to communicate and work together, which can reduce the efficiency and effectiveness of the network.

5. Decentralization: Sharding can also have implications for decentralization. In a sharded network, each shard is essentially a smaller, independent network. This means that power and control may become more centralized within individual shards, which could undermine the decentralization of the network as a whole.

Overall, while sharding can offer significant benefits in terms of scalability, it is not a silver bullet solution and must be carefully implemented and managed to ensure its effectiveness and security.

## Chapter 2: Cross-Chain Interoperability
## The importance of interoperability between different blockchain networks

Interoperability is a critical aspect of blockchain technology that has the potential to revolutionize the way value is exchanged between different networks. In essence, interoperability refers to the ability of different blockchain networks to communicate and interact with each other seamlessly, without the need for intermediaries. This is important because, currently, most blockchain networks operate in isolation, with limited or no ability to communicate with each other. This limits the scope and utility of blockchain technology, as it makes it difficult for users to exchange value between different networks, and for developers to create applications that span multiple networks.

There are several reasons why interoperability is important for the blockchain ecosystem. First, it enables users to access a wider range of assets and services, regardless of which network they are hosted on. For example, if a user wants to trade an asset that is only available on a particular blockchain network, they would typically have to convert it into a more widely accepted asset, such as Bitcoin or Ethereum, before they can trade it on a different network. This process can be time-consuming, costly, and inefficient, and can create friction in the blockchain ecosystem.

Second, interoperability enables developers to create more sophisticated and powerful applications that span multiple networks. For example, a decentralized finance (DeFi) application that allows users to trade, lend, and borrow assets across multiple networks would be much more powerful and flexible than one that is limited to a single network. Similarly, a supply chain management application that spans multiple networks could provide greater visibility and transparency into the movement of goods and services, reducing costs and improving efficiency.

Finally, interoperability promotes competition and innovation in the blockchain ecosystem, by enabling different networks to compete and collaborate with each other. This can lead to the development of new and innovative blockchain applications and services, as well as the emergence of new blockchain networks that offer unique features and capabilities.

Overall, interoperability is a critical aspect of blockchain technology that has the potential to unlock significant value and drive innovation in the blockchain ecosystem. As such, it is essential that developers and stakeholders in the blockchain community work towards developing robust and reliable cross-chain interoperability solutions that enable seamless communication and interaction between different blockchain networks.

## An overview of existing cross-chain solutions, such as atomic swaps and wrapped tokens

Cross-chain interoperability is an essential aspect of blockchain technology that enables different blockchain networks to communicate and exchange value with each other. There are various cross-chain solutions available, each with its own set of advantages and disadvantages. In this chapter, we will provide an overview of some of the most popular cross-chain solutions, such as atomic swaps and wrapped tokens.

Atomic Swaps

Atomic swaps are a decentralized way of exchanging cryptocurrencies between different blockchain networks without the need for an intermediary. Atomic swaps are trustless and secure because they use smart contracts that ensure the exchange of assets occurs only when the conditions of the contract are met.

The basic principle of atomic swaps is that two parties agree to exchange a specific amount of cryptocurrency, such as Bitcoin and Litecoin, without the need for a centralized exchange. Atomic swaps work by creating a hash time-locked contract (HTLC) on both blockchain networks, which means that the transaction is only valid if certain conditions are met, such as the receiving party confirming receipt of the cryptocurrency.

One advantage of atomic swaps is that they eliminate the need for a centralized exchange, which reduces the risk of hacking and fraud. Atomic swaps are also more private than centralized exchanges because they do not require users to disclose their personal information. However, atomic swaps can be more complicated to execute than traditional exchanges and require some technical expertise.

Wrapped Tokens

Wrapped tokens are another type of cross-chain solution that enable cryptocurrencies to be transferred between different blockchain networks. Wrapped tokens are created by locking up an underlying cryptocurrency, such as Bitcoin or Ethereum, and issuing an equivalent token on a different blockchain network, such as the Binance Smart Chain.

Wrapped tokens enable the seamless transfer of assets between different blockchain networks, which is particularly useful for decentralized finance (DeFi) applications that require access to multiple blockchain networks. Wrapped tokens also enable the use of cryptocurrencies as collateral in DeFi applications, which was not possible before.

One disadvantage of wrapped tokens is that they are not as decentralized as atomic swaps because they require the use of a custodian to hold the underlying cryptocurrency. The custodian is responsible for creating and destroying the wrapped tokens, which creates a single point of failure. However, some wrapped token solutions have implemented multisig custodianship, which increases security by requiring multiple parties to authorize transactions.

Conclusion

Cross-chain interoperability is a crucial aspect of blockchain technology that enables different blockchain networks to communicate and exchange value with each other. Atomic swaps and wrapped tokens are two popular cross-chain solutions that offer unique advantages and disadvantages. As the blockchain ecosystem continues to evolve, new cross-chain solutions will emerge, enabling even greater interoperability between different blockchain networks.

## The potential impact of cross-chain interoperability on the blockchain ecosystem

The potential impact of cross-chain interoperability on the blockchain ecosystem is significant, and it could transform the way we use and interact with blockchain networks. Here are some potential impacts of cross-chain interoperability:

1. Improved Liquidity: Cross-chain interoperability can enable the transfer of assets between different blockchain networks, which could significantly improve liquidity for these assets. This is because it would allow users to trade assets across different blockchain networks, which could lead to increased trading volume and liquidity.

2. Enhanced Functionality: Cross-chain interoperability can enable developers to create more complex and advanced applications that can interact with multiple blockchain networks. This can lead to the creation of new use cases and applications that were not previously possible.

3. Increased Security: Cross-chain interoperability can enable blockchain networks to collaborate and share security features, such as consensus algorithms, to improve security across the entire ecosystem. This can reduce the risk of 51%

attacks and other security threats that could harm the blockchain ecosystem.

4. Improved Decentralization: Cross-chain interoperability can enable the creation of more decentralized applications and networks by allowing users to access resources from multiple blockchain networks. This can reduce the reliance on a single network and improve the overall decentralization of the blockchain ecosystem.

5. Reduced Transaction Fees: Cross-chain interoperability can enable users to transfer assets between different blockchain networks at a lower cost than traditional methods. This can reduce transaction fees and make blockchain networks more accessible to a wider range of users.

Overall, cross-chain interoperability has the potential to transform the blockchain ecosystem by enabling more complex applications, increasing liquidity, improving security, and reducing transaction fees. It is an essential innovation that will play a significant role in the future of blockchain technology.

# Chapter 3: Zero-Knowledge Proofs and Privacy
## An introduction to zero-knowledge proofs and their role in preserving privacy on the blockchain

Zero-knowledge proofs (ZKPs) are a cryptographic tool that allow parties to prove the authenticity of information without revealing any underlying data. This means that a prover can convince a verifier that they know a piece of information, without actually revealing what that information is. ZKPs have a variety of applications, but one area where they have shown great promise is in preserving privacy on the blockchain.

Privacy is a crucial concern for many blockchain users, as the transparency of the blockchain means that all transactions are publicly visible. This lack of privacy can be problematic for users who want to keep their financial activities private, or who don't want their personal information to be exposed. ZKPs offer a way to maintain privacy while still ensuring the integrity of the blockchain.

At a high level, ZKPs work by enabling a prover to convince a verifier that a certain statement is true, without revealing any information about the statement itself. This is accomplished by breaking down the statement into a series of mathematical equations, and then using a combination of randomness and encryption to hide the underlying information.

One common type of ZKP is the zero-knowledge proof of knowledge (ZKPK), which is used to prove that the prover knows a certain secret value. This can be used to authenticate users on the blockchain without requiring them to reveal their private keys. Another type of ZKP is the zero-knowledge proof of membership (ZKPM), which can be used to prove that a particular piece of data is included in a certain set without revealing any other information about the set.

ZKPs have a number of potential applications in blockchain security beyond privacy preservation. For example, they can be used to improve the efficiency of smart contracts by enabling verifiers to check the validity of a contract without having to execute it. They can also be used to ensure that certain conditions are met before a transaction is executed, such as ensuring that a user is of a certain age before allowing them to purchase alcohol.

Overall, ZKPs are a powerful tool for preserving privacy and improving security on the blockchain. As blockchain technology continues to evolve, it is likely that we will see more and more applications of ZKPs in the future.

## Examples of blockchain networks that use zero-knowledge proofs, such as Zcash

Zero-knowledge proofs (ZKPs) are a cryptographic technique that allows one party to prove to another party that a certain statement is true, without revealing any additional information beyond the statement's truthfulness. This property makes ZKPs a valuable tool for maintaining privacy and confidentiality in a wide range of applications, including blockchain networks.

One of the most well-known examples of a blockchain network that uses ZKPs is Zcash. Launched in 2016, Zcash is a privacy-focused cryptocurrency that aims to provide users with the option to conduct completely anonymous transactions. To achieve this goal, Zcash uses a specific type of ZKP known as a zk-SNARK (zero-knowledge succinct non-interactive argument of knowledge).

In the Zcash network, users can choose to send either transparent transactions, which function like traditional cryptocurrency transactions and are recorded on the blockchain for public viewing, or shielded transactions, which are completely private and use zk-SNARKs to prove their validity without revealing any additional information. This means that the sender, receiver, and amount of a shielded transaction are all hidden from public view.

The use of ZKPs in Zcash has led to some controversy within the cryptocurrency community. Some critics argue that the option for completely anonymous transactions could facilitate illegal activities, such as money laundering or terrorism financing. However, supporters of Zcash counter that the privacy features are an important tool for protecting the personal information of everyday users who may not want their financial transactions visible to the public.

In addition to Zcash, other blockchain networks are also exploring the use of ZKPs to preserve privacy. For example, the Ethereum network is currently working on a ZKP-based solution called Aztec Protocol, which aims to enable private transactions and smart contracts on the Ethereum blockchain.

Overall, the use of ZKPs represents an important area of innovation in blockchain technology, offering new possibilities for maintaining privacy and confidentiality in decentralized networks. While there are certainly challenges and limitations to be addressed in the implementation of ZKPs, the potential benefits they offer for users and the blockchain ecosystem as a whole make them an exciting area to watch in the coming years.

## The potential impact of zero-knowledge proofs on the broader technology landscape

Zero-knowledge proofs (ZKPs) have the potential to revolutionize the way we approach privacy and security in various industries, not just blockchain. In this section, we will discuss the potential impact of ZKPs on the broader technology landscape.

1. Improved Privacy ZKPs have the potential to improve privacy in a wide range of industries, including finance, healthcare, and government. With the use of ZKPs, individuals can prove certain facts about themselves or their assets without revealing any additional information. This technology can help protect personal data while still allowing for verification and validation.

2. Enhanced Security ZKPs can also enhance security by preventing data breaches and other malicious activities. For example, ZKPs can be used to create secure logins without revealing sensitive user data. This would prevent hackers from stealing user passwords or other sensitive information.

3. Greater Trust ZKPs can also help build trust between parties by allowing for more transparent and auditable transactions. For example, in supply chain management, ZKPs can be used to ensure the authenticity

and quality of products. This technology can also help prevent fraud and other illicit activities.

4. New Applications ZKPs are still a relatively new technology, and as such, we are only beginning to understand their full potential. As more use cases emerge, we may see entirely new applications of this technology that we haven't yet considered. For example, ZKPs could be used in voting systems to ensure the integrity of elections while maintaining voter privacy.

5. Broader Adoption As the benefits of ZKPs become more widely recognized, we can expect to see broader adoption of this technology across various industries. This could lead to new business models and revenue streams, as well as greater efficiency and cost savings.

6. Potential Challenges Despite the many benefits of ZKPs, there are also potential challenges to consider. For example, the use of ZKPs could increase the complexity of systems, which could make it more difficult to develop and maintain these systems. Additionally, there could be regulatory challenges related to the use of ZKPs in certain industries.

In conclusion, zero-knowledge proofs have the potential to have a significant impact on the broader technology landscape. This technology has the potential to improve privacy, enhance security, build trust, and lead to new applications and greater adoption. However, there are also potential challenges to consider as this technology continues to evolve and mature.

## Chapter 4: Quantum Computing and Blockchain Security

### An overview of quantum computing and its potential impact on blockchain security

Quantum computing has been a rapidly evolving field in recent years, with significant advances being made in both hardware and software development. It is a type of computing that is based on the principles of quantum mechanics, which allow for the creation of powerful computing machines that can solve problems that are impossible for classical computers.

Quantum computers use qubits, which are units of information that are analogous to classical bits but can exist in multiple states simultaneously. This ability to be in multiple states at once enables quantum computers to perform certain types of computations much more efficiently than classical computers. However, this also means that quantum computers can potentially break the encryption schemes that are used to secure many of the world's computer systems, including blockchain networks.

Quantum computing's potential impact on blockchain security is a significant concern for the industry. Many blockchain networks use encryption algorithms that are currently considered secure against classical computers but could be vulnerable to quantum computers. As quantum computing technology continues to develop, it is becoming increasingly important to explore and develop new encryption schemes that are resistant to quantum attacks.

One of the primary encryption schemes used in blockchain networks is the Elliptic Curve Digital Signature Algorithm (ECDSA), which is used to generate public and private keys for digital signatures. The security of ECDSA relies on the difficulty of solving certain mathematical problems, which are known as the discrete logarithm problem and the elliptic curve discrete logarithm problem. However, quantum computers can solve these problems efficiently using Shor's algorithm, which could potentially compromise the security of blockchain networks.

To address this issue, researchers and developers are exploring new encryption schemes that are resistant to quantum attacks. One promising approach is to use post-quantum cryptography, which refers to encryption algorithms that are designed to be resistant to attacks by both classical and quantum computers. Some examples of post-quantum cryptographic algorithms include hash-based signatures, lattice-based signatures, and code-based cryptography.

Another potential solution to the threat posed by quantum computers is to develop quantum-resistant blockchain networks. These networks would be designed from the ground up to be resistant to quantum attacks, using encryption schemes that are specifically designed to be secure against quantum computers. Some examples of quantum-resistant blockchain networks that are currently being developed include QAN Platform, Quantum Resistant Ledger (QRL), and Qubitica.

In addition to the threat posed by quantum computing, there are other potential security risks that blockchain networks face, such as 51% attacks and Sybil attacks. These attacks can compromise the integrity and security of the network, potentially leading to the loss of funds and other sensitive information. To address these threats, blockchain networks are implementing various security measures, such as proof-of-work and proof-of-stake consensus algorithms, and multi-party computation (MPC) protocols.

Conclusion

Quantum computing has the potential to significantly impact blockchain security, as many of the encryption algorithms used in blockchain networks could be vulnerable to quantum attacks. However, there are various approaches that can be taken to address this issue, such as post-quantum cryptography and quantum-resistant blockchain networks. It is essential for the blockchain industry to continue to explore and develop new security measures to protect against the evolving threat landscape and ensure the integrity and security of blockchain networks.

## Existing efforts to develop quantum-resistant blockchain solutions

Quantum computing is a rapidly evolving field that poses a significant threat to the security of traditional cryptographic systems. As the power of quantum computers continues to grow, many experts believe that traditional cryptographic algorithms will become vulnerable to attacks that can break even the strongest encryption.

To address this challenge, researchers are actively exploring new approaches to cryptography that are resistant to quantum attacks. In the context of blockchain, quantum-resistant cryptography is becoming an increasingly important area of research, as it is critical to maintaining the security and integrity of distributed ledger systems.

One of the most promising approaches to quantum-resistant cryptography is lattice-based cryptography. Lattice-based cryptography relies on the properties of mathematical objects called lattices, which are essentially grids of points in space. By leveraging the properties of lattices, researchers have been able to develop cryptographic algorithms that are resistant to quantum attacks.

Another approach to quantum-resistant cryptography is hash-based cryptography. Hash-based cryptography is based on the properties of hash functions, which are mathematical functions that convert arbitrary data into fixed-size output. By using hash functions, it is possible to construct cryptographic protocols that are resistant to quantum attacks.

Several blockchain projects are already working on developing quantum-resistant cryptographic solutions. One notable example is the Quantum Resistant Ledger (QRL), which is a blockchain that uses hash-based cryptography to provide quantum-resistant security. The QRL is designed to be resistant to all known quantum attacks, including attacks that use the Shor's algorithm to break traditional cryptographic systems.

Another example is the IOTA project, which uses a quantum-resistant signature scheme called Winternitz One-Time Signatures (WOTS). WOTS is a hash-based signature scheme that is resistant to quantum attacks, and it has been integrated into the IOTA protocol to provide quantum-resistant security.

In addition to these projects, there are several other blockchain initiatives that are exploring quantum-resistant cryptography. For example, the Hyperledger project has a working group dedicated to researching quantum-safe cryptography for distributed ledger systems.

Overall, the development of quantum-resistant blockchain solutions is an active area of research, and there are many promising approaches being explored. As the threat of quantum computing continues to grow, it is essential that blockchain projects prioritize the development of quantum-resistant security solutions to ensure the long-term viability and security of distributed ledger systems.

## The potential implications of quantum computing for the broader technology landscape

Quantum computing is an emerging technology that has the potential to revolutionize many fields, including cryptography and information security. While quantum computers have not yet reached the level of maturity to pose a significant threat to blockchain security, the potential implications for the broader technology landscape are significant.

One of the most significant implications of quantum computing is its ability to break many of the cryptographic algorithms that are currently used to secure information. This includes the elliptic curve cryptography (ECC) that is used in many blockchain networks. Quantum computers can solve certain mathematical problems much faster than classical computers, making it possible to break these algorithms in a matter of minutes or even seconds.

The potential impact of quantum computing on blockchain security has been the subject of much discussion in the industry. While some experts believe that quantum computing could render many blockchain networks vulnerable to attack, others argue that the development of quantum-resistant algorithms could help to mitigate this threat.

One approach to developing quantum-resistant blockchain solutions is to use post-quantum cryptography, which is designed to be secure against both classical and quantum computers. There are several post-quantum cryptography algorithms that have been proposed, including lattice-based cryptography and code-based cryptography. These algorithms rely on mathematical problems that are believed to be hard for both classical and quantum computers to solve.

Another approach to developing quantum-resistant blockchain solutions is to use quantum cryptography. This involves using the principles of quantum mechanics to secure information, such as by using quantum key distribution to securely share cryptographic keys between two parties. While quantum cryptography is still in the experimental phase, it has the potential to be a highly secure solution for blockchain networks in the future.

The development of quantum-resistant blockchain solutions is important not only for the security of blockchain networks, but also for the broader technology landscape. As quantum computing continues to evolve, it will become increasingly important to have secure cryptographic algorithms that can withstand the power of quantum computers. This will require significant research and development efforts in the field of cryptography, as well as the integration of these solutions into blockchain networks.

In addition to the development of quantum-resistant blockchain solutions, there are other potential implications of quantum computing for the broader technology landscape. For example, quantum computers could be used to break into secure communication channels, such as those used by government agencies and financial institutions. This could have significant implications for national security and financial stability.

On the other hand, quantum computing could also enable new breakthroughs in fields such as drug discovery, materials science, and artificial intelligence. This could lead to significant advancements in a wide range of industries, including healthcare, manufacturing, and finance.

In conclusion, quantum computing has the potential to be a disruptive force in the technology landscape, with significant implications for blockchain security and other fields. While the development of quantum-resistant blockchain solutions is still in its early stages, it is clear that this will be an important area of research in the coming years. By working to develop secure and resilient blockchain networks, we can help to ensure that the benefits of blockchain technology are realized in a safe and secure manner.

## Chapter 5: Decentralized Governance and Security
### The importance of decentralized governance for ensuring blockchain security

Decentralized governance is an essential aspect of blockchain technology. It involves a decentralized decision-making process, where decisions are made by consensus among stakeholders instead of a central authority. Decentralized governance ensures the security and integrity of the blockchain by ensuring that no single entity or group can make unilateral decisions that can undermine the network's security.

Decentralized governance is crucial for blockchain security in several ways. Firstly, it ensures that decisions that affect the network's security are made in a transparent and democratic manner. This transparency ensures that all stakeholders have a say in the decisions that affect the network's security, reducing the likelihood of malicious actors making decisions that can harm the network.

Secondly, decentralized governance ensures that the blockchain network remains resistant to attacks. Since there is no central point of control, it becomes difficult for attackers to compromise the network's security. The network's security is maintained by a distributed network of nodes, making it harder for attackers to take control of the network.

Decentralized governance also promotes innovation in blockchain security. Since decisions are made through a consensus mechanism, stakeholders are encouraged to come up with new ideas and proposals that can improve the network's security. This innovation helps to keep the network secure and resilient to new threats.

An example of a blockchain network that uses decentralized governance is Ethereum. Ethereum has a decentralized decision-making process where decisions are made by its stakeholders through a consensus mechanism called Proof of Stake (PoS). Under PoS, stakeholders can vote on proposed changes to the network, and these changes are implemented if they receive sufficient support.

Decentralized governance also plays a critical role in ensuring the network's continued growth and development. Since decisions are made through consensus, it becomes easier for the network to adapt to changing circumstances and incorporate new technologies that can improve its security.

In conclusion, decentralized governance is an essential aspect of blockchain security. It ensures that decisions that affect the network's security are made in a transparent and democratic manner, promotes innovation in blockchain security, and ensures that the network remains resilient to attacks. As blockchain technology continues to evolve, decentralized governance will play an increasingly critical role in ensuring its continued security and growth.

## An overview of existing decentralized governance solutions, such as DAOs

Decentralized autonomous organizations (DAOs) are a type of decentralized governance solution that have gained popularity in recent years, particularly in the blockchain space. DAOs are essentially organizations that are run by code and governed by their members, rather than by a centralized authority or board of directors.

DAOs typically have a set of rules or smart contracts that govern how they operate and make decisions. These rules may include how new members are admitted, how proposals are submitted and voted on, and how funds are allocated. The code that powers a DAO is open-source and transparent, meaning that anyone can audit the code and verify that it is working as intended.

One of the key benefits of DAOs is that they can be highly transparent and democratic. Because all members have a say in decision-making, and all decisions are recorded on the blockchain, there is little room for corruption or manipulation. This can be particularly important in contexts where trust is low or where there is a need for accountability and transparency.

There are already a number of successful DAOs in existence, including MakerDAO, which governs the Dai stablecoin, and MolochDAO, which provides funding for Ethereum ecosystem projects. These DAOs have shown that it is possible to create functional, decentralized organizations that can operate at scale.

However, there are also challenges associated with DAOs. One of the key challenges is that they can be difficult to govern effectively. Because decisions are made through a decentralized voting process, it can be hard to reach consensus or to ensure that all members are acting in the best interests of the organization. Additionally, DAOs may be vulnerable to attacks or exploits that take advantage of vulnerabilities in their smart contracts.

Despite these challenges, DAOs represent an important development in the evolution of decentralized governance solutions. As blockchain technology continues to mature, it is likely that we will see more and more organizations adopting DAO-like structures to improve transparency, accountability, and efficiency.

## The potential impact of decentralized governance on the blockchain ecosystem

Decentralized governance, also known as self-governance or community governance, is an emerging trend in the blockchain ecosystem. It involves giving the community of users and stakeholders in a blockchain network the power to make decisions about the network's operations, including its security.

The potential impact of decentralized governance on the blockchain ecosystem is significant. It could lead to a more democratic and transparent system, where decisions are made by a diverse group of stakeholders instead of a central authority. This, in turn, could lead to a more resilient and secure blockchain network.

One potential impact of decentralized governance is the ability to prevent centralized control and manipulation of the network. With centralized governance, a single entity or group of entities has the power to make decisions about the network, which can lead to conflicts of interest and a lack of transparency. Decentralized governance, on the other hand, distributes decision-making power among the community of users and stakeholders, preventing any single entity from dominating the network.

Another potential impact of decentralized governance is the ability to promote community participation and engagement. When users and stakeholders have a say in the network's operations, they are more likely to be invested in its success and more likely to actively participate in its growth and development. This can lead to a more vibrant and engaged community, which can, in turn, contribute to the network's overall security and resilience.

Decentralized governance also has the potential to promote innovation and experimentation. When decision-making power is distributed among a diverse group of stakeholders, there is more room for new ideas and approaches to be explored. This can lead to a more dynamic and innovative blockchain ecosystem, which can, in turn, lead to better security and resilience.

However, there are also potential challenges and drawbacks to decentralized governance. For example, it can be difficult to reach consensus among a large and diverse group of stakeholders, which can lead to delays or conflicts. Additionally, there is always the risk of bad actors infiltrating the network and attempting to manipulate the decision-making process.

Overall, the potential impact of decentralized governance on the blockchain ecosystem is significant. While there are challenges and potential drawbacks, the benefits of a more democratic, transparent, and engaged community of users and stakeholders are clear. As the blockchain ecosystem continues to evolve and grow, decentralized governance will likely play an increasingly important role in ensuring the security and resilience of these networks.

## Chapter 6: Regulatory Compliance and Security
## The importance of regulatory compliance for ensuring blockchain security

Blockchain technology has the potential to revolutionize many industries by providing a secure, transparent, and decentralized system for storing and transferring data. However, the decentralized nature of blockchain also poses challenges for regulatory compliance. In this chapter, we will explore the importance of regulatory compliance for ensuring blockchain security and the challenges that arise when trying to achieve it.

The concept of regulatory compliance refers to the adherence of individuals, organizations, and institutions to a set of laws, rules, and regulations that have been put in place to ensure the safety, security, and transparency of various industries. These regulations can come from government agencies, industry bodies, or other regulatory bodies. In the context of blockchain technology, regulatory compliance is particularly important because it helps to prevent fraud, money laundering, and other illicit activities.

One of the biggest challenges of regulatory compliance in blockchain technology is the decentralized nature of the blockchain network. Because blockchain is a distributed ledger that is maintained by a network of nodes, it can be difficult to enforce regulations and ensure that all nodes are complying with the same set of rules. Additionally, blockchain transactions are pseudonymous, which can make it challenging to trace transactions back to their source and verify the identity of the parties involved.

Despite these challenges, there are several initiatives underway to improve regulatory compliance in the blockchain ecosystem. One such initiative is the development of blockchain-based identity verification systems that can help to verify the identity of users on the blockchain network. By verifying the identity of users, it becomes easier to enforce regulatory compliance and prevent illicit activities.

Another initiative is the development of blockchain-based regulatory sandboxes. These sandboxes provide a safe and controlled environment for blockchain companies to test new products and services while complying with regulatory requirements. This approach allows companies to innovate while still adhering to regulatory standards.

Regulatory compliance is also important for the adoption of blockchain technology in traditional industries such as finance and healthcare. These industries are heavily regulated, and blockchain technology must comply with the same regulations as traditional systems. Failure to comply with these regulations can result in significant fines and reputational damage.

To address these challenges, there have been efforts to create blockchain-based regulatory solutions. For example, blockchain technology can be used to automate compliance processes, reducing the risk of human error and increasing efficiency. Additionally, blockchain can be used to create a tamper-proof record of regulatory compliance, making it easier to audit and enforce compliance.

In conclusion, regulatory compliance is critical for ensuring the security of the blockchain ecosystem. While there are challenges to achieving regulatory compliance in a decentralized network, there are also several initiatives underway to improve compliance and ensure that blockchain technology can be used in a safe and transparent manner. By working together, industry participants, regulators, and other stakeholders can create a regulatory framework that promotes innovation while ensuring the safety and security of the blockchain ecosystem.

## An overview of existing regulatory frameworks for blockchain technology, such as the FATF guidelines

Introduction Blockchain technology has the potential to revolutionize industries across the globe, but with its benefits come challenges such as regulatory compliance. As with any technology, blockchain systems must adhere to local, national, and international laws to ensure their security and longevity. In this chapter, we will explore the importance of regulatory compliance for blockchain security and provide an overview of existing regulatory frameworks for blockchain technology.

Importance of Regulatory Compliance for Blockchain Security Blockchain technology operates on a decentralized platform that allows for peer-to-peer transactions, eliminating the need for intermediaries. However, this lack of intermediaries and centralized oversight can present challenges when it comes to regulatory compliance. Without proper regulations, blockchain systems may be used for illicit activities, such as money laundering or terrorism financing. Furthermore, the lack of regulatory compliance may result in a loss of trust in the blockchain system, leading to a decrease in adoption and investment.

In addition, regulatory compliance is essential for protecting investors and consumers. Regulatory frameworks provide rules and guidelines for initial coin offerings (ICOs) and other cryptocurrency transactions, ensuring that investors are not exposed to fraudulent activities. Additionally, regulatory frameworks can protect consumers by ensuring that blockchain-based products and services are safe and secure.

Existing Regulatory Frameworks for Blockchain Technology As blockchain technology becomes more prevalent, many countries are developing regulatory frameworks to address the unique challenges that come with this technology. The following are some of the existing regulatory frameworks for blockchain technology.

Financial Action Task Force (FATF) The Financial Action Task Force (FATF) is an intergovernmental organization that was established to combat money laundering and terrorism financing. In 2019, the FATF issued guidance on virtual assets and virtual asset service providers (VASPs), providing a framework for countries to regulate cryptocurrency transactions. The FATF guidelines require VASPs to adhere to anti-money laundering (AML) and counter-terrorism financing (CTF) regulations.

European Union (EU) The European Union (EU) has been proactive in developing regulatory frameworks for blockchain technology. In 2018, the European Parliament passed the General Data Protection Regulation (GDPR), which provides a framework for protecting personal data. The GDPR applies to blockchain technology, as it contains personal data. Additionally, the EU has been developing regulations for ICOs, cryptocurrency exchanges, and wallets.

United States (US) In the United States, regulatory frameworks for blockchain technology vary by state. The Securities and Exchange Commission (SEC) has been active in regulating ICOs, considering many to be securities. Additionally, the Commodity Futures Trading Commission (CFTC) has been active in regulating cryptocurrency derivatives. In 2019, the CFTC issued guidance on cryptocurrency derivatives, providing a framework for their regulation.

China China has been developing regulatory frameworks for blockchain technology since 2016. In 2019, the country passed a cryptography law, which provides a framework for regulating cryptography technologies, including blockchain. Additionally, China has been developing regulations for ICOs, cryptocurrency exchanges, and wallets.

The Potential Impact of Regulatory Compliance on the Blockchain Ecosystem Regulatory compliance is essential for the long-term success and adoption of blockchain technology. Compliance provides legitimacy and credibility to blockchain-based products and services, which may lead to increased adoption and investment. Furthermore, regulatory compliance can protect investors and consumers, ensuring that they are not exposed to fraudulent activities.

However, regulatory compliance can also present challenges for blockchain technology. Compliance may increase costs and decrease the speed of innovation. Additionally, compliance can limit the ability of blockchain systems to operate globally, as regulations may differ by country.

Conclusion Regulatory compliance is essential for ensuring the security and longevity of blockchain technology. Compliance provides rules and guidelines for ICOs, cryptocurrency transactions, and other blockchain-based activities, protecting investors and consumers from fraudulent activities. However, compliance can also present challenges, including increased costs and complexity for blockchain-based companies. Compliance requirements can vary widely by jurisdiction, and keeping up with regulatory changes can be difficult. Additionally, some blockchain applications may be inherently difficult to regulate due to their decentralized nature. Despite these challenges, regulatory compliance is necessary for the blockchain industry to gain wider acceptance and adoption, particularly in the context of institutional investment and mainstream use cases.

      One of the most notable regulatory frameworks for blockchain technology is the set of guidelines issued by the Financial Action Task Force (FATF). The FATF is an intergovernmental organization that develops and promotes policies to combat money laundering and terrorist financing. In 2019, the FATF issued guidance for virtual asset service providers (VASPs), including exchanges and wallet providers, to comply with anti-money laundering and counter-terrorism financing regulations. The guidance requires VASPs to collect and share customer information, conduct risk assessments, and report suspicious activity to regulatory authorities. While the guidelines are not binding, many countries have implemented them in their regulatory frameworks, and non-compliant companies risk being shut out of global markets. Other regulatory frameworks for blockchain technology include the EU's General Data Protection Regulation (GDPR), the US Securities and Exchange Commission (SEC), and the Chinese government's crackdown on cryptocurrency trading and mining activities.

## The potential impact of regulatory compliance on the broader technology landscape

Blockchain technology has the potential to transform numerous industries, but its adoption is highly dependent on regulatory compliance. As blockchain continues to gain traction, governments around the world are grappling with how to regulate this technology while balancing innovation and consumer protection. The potential impact of regulatory compliance on the broader technology landscape is significant and multifaceted, with both positive and negative consequences.

One potential positive impact of regulatory compliance is increased adoption of blockchain technology by traditional financial institutions. Many banks and financial institutions have been hesitant to adopt blockchain technology due to concerns over regulatory compliance. However, as regulatory frameworks are established and compliance becomes more standardized, financial institutions may be more willing to adopt blockchain technology and explore new business models, which could ultimately lead to increased efficiency and cost savings for consumers.

Additionally, regulatory compliance can also help to address concerns over fraud and illicit activity in the blockchain space. By establishing clear guidelines and regulations, governments can help to mitigate the risks associated with ICOs, cryptocurrency transactions, and other blockchain-based activities. This increased transparency and accountability could help to build trust in the technology and encourage wider adoption.

However, there are also potential negative impacts of regulatory compliance on the broader technology landscape. One concern is that overly burdensome regulations could stifle innovation and prevent new blockchain-based businesses from emerging. Compliance can be a costly and time-consuming process, which could make it more difficult for startups and smaller companies to compete with established players in the market.

Furthermore, regulatory compliance could also lead to fragmentation in the blockchain space. Different regulatory frameworks across different jurisdictions could create a patchwork of regulations that make it difficult for blockchain companies to operate across borders. This could ultimately limit the potential of blockchain technology to achieve global adoption and interoperability.

In conclusion, regulatory compliance is a critical factor in the adoption and success of blockchain technology. While there are potential benefits to establishing clear guidelines and regulations, there are also potential negative impacts that must be carefully considered. Finding the right balance between innovation and regulation will be essential for ensuring the long-term viability and success of blockchain technology.

# Chapter 7: Investment and Innovation in Blockchain Security

## An overview of investment trends and emerging players in the blockchain security space

As blockchain technology continues to gain popularity and wider adoption, the importance of securing it has become more apparent. With billions of dollars at stake, it is no surprise that investment in blockchain security has grown significantly in recent years. In this chapter, we will provide an overview of investment trends and emerging players in the blockchain security space.

Investment in blockchain security is on the rise, with venture capitalists and institutional investors pouring millions of dollars into promising startups and established players in the industry. According to a report by CB Insights, investment in blockchain security companies reached a record high of $788 million in 2020, up from $481 million in 2019. This trend is expected to continue in the coming years, as more companies and governments recognize the importance of securing their blockchain-based systems.

Some of the top players in the blockchain security space include traditional cybersecurity companies like IBM and McAfee, as well as blockchain-specific security companies such as Chainalysis, CipherTrace, and BitGo.

These companies offer a range of solutions, including anti-money laundering (AML) and know your customer (KYC) compliance tools, fraud detection and prevention, and secure custody solutions.

In addition to established players, there are also a number of promising startups emerging in the blockchain security space. These startups are focused on addressing some of the most pressing security issues facing the blockchain industry, including quantum computing threats, decentralized governance, and smart contract vulnerabilities.

One such startup is QAN Platform, which is building a quantum-resistant blockchain platform that utilizes post-quantum cryptography to protect against quantum computing threats. Another startup, Aragon, is focused on decentralized governance, providing tools for creating and managing decentralized autonomous organizations (DAOs) on the blockchain.

Other notable blockchain security startups include CertiK, which provides formal verification solutions to ensure the security of smart contracts, and Unbound Tech, which offers a range of security solutions, including secure multi-party computation and secure key management.

In addition to venture capital investment, governments and large corporations are also investing in blockchain security research and development. For example, the US government has allocated significant resources to researching and developing blockchain security solutions, while companies like Microsoft and IBM are investing in blockchain security research in order to stay ahead of emerging threats.

Overall, the investment and innovation in blockchain security is a positive sign for the industry. As more resources are devoted to securing blockchain-based systems, the technology will become more secure and resilient, paving the way for wider adoption and further innovation.

## The potential impact of continued innovation on the blockchain security landscape

Blockchain security is a constantly evolving field, with new threats and vulnerabilities emerging all the time. The importance of continued investment and innovation in blockchain security cannot be overstated, as it is critical for the long-term success and adoption of blockchain technology.

One area where continued innovation could have a significant impact is in the development of more advanced encryption and cryptographic techniques. As we have seen, quantum computing has the potential to break many of the encryption techniques used in blockchain today, and as such, it is important to develop quantum-resistant cryptographic solutions. This is an area where significant investment is currently being made, with research into post-quantum cryptography and other quantum-resistant techniques.

Another area where continued innovation could have an impact is in the development of new consensus mechanisms. While proof-of-work has been the dominant consensus mechanism for many years, it is becoming increasingly clear that it is not sustainable in the long term, due to its high energy consumption and environmental impact. As a result, many blockchain projects are exploring alternative consensus mechanisms, such as proof-of-stake, delegated proof-of-stake, and other variations. These consensus mechanisms have the potential to be more energy-efficient and environmentally sustainable, while still providing the necessary security guarantees.

Furthermore, continued innovation in areas such as zero-knowledge proofs, cross-chain interoperability, and decentralized governance could also have a significant impact on the blockchain security landscape. For example, the use of zero-knowledge proofs could allow for greater privacy and anonymity on the blockchain, while cross-chain interoperability could enable more seamless and secure transactions between different blockchain networks. Decentralized governance solutions such as DAOs could also help to ensure greater security and transparency in blockchain projects.

In addition to these areas of innovation, continued investment in blockchain security research and development is critical to stay ahead of new and emerging threats. This includes investment in both technical and non-technical solutions, such as security audits, penetration testing, and other risk management strategies. As blockchain technology becomes more widely adopted, it is likely that we will see an increase in both the sophistication and frequency of attacks, making continued investment in blockchain security even more important.

Overall, the potential impact of continued innovation on the blockchain security landscape is significant. By investing in new and emerging technologies, we can help to ensure the long-term success and adoption of blockchain, while also providing greater security and protection for users and investors. As such, it is essential that we continue to support and encourage investment and innovation in this critical area.

## Opportunities and challenges for entrepreneurs and investors in the blockchain security space

As blockchain technology continues to mature and gain wider adoption, the need for effective security solutions will only increase. This presents a unique opportunity for entrepreneurs and investors to develop innovative blockchain security solutions that can help to secure the ecosystem and drive further growth. However, this also comes with a number of challenges that must be overcome.

One of the main challenges for entrepreneurs and investors in the blockchain security space is the constantly evolving nature of the technology. As new use cases and applications emerge, new security challenges will also arise, requiring innovative solutions that can adapt and evolve over time.

Another challenge is the regulatory landscape, which can be difficult to navigate for startups and investors alike. Compliance with regulatory requirements is essential for success in the blockchain security space, but can be expensive and time-consuming, especially for smaller startups with limited resources.

In addition, there is intense competition in the blockchain security market, with many established players and well-funded startups vying for a share of the market.

This makes it more difficult for new entrants to gain traction and compete effectively.

Despite these challenges, there are also significant opportunities for entrepreneurs and investors in the blockchain security space. For example, the increasing number of high-profile security breaches and hacks has raised awareness of the importance of blockchain security, creating a growing demand for effective solutions.

In addition, the decentralized nature of blockchain technology means that there is a need for new types of security solutions that are specifically tailored to the unique challenges of this ecosystem. This presents an opportunity for innovative startups to develop new solutions that can meet these needs and differentiate themselves from competitors.

Another opportunity is the potential for blockchain technology to disrupt traditional industries and create new business models. This can create new opportunities for startups and investors to provide innovative security solutions that can help to secure these emerging markets.

To succeed in the blockchain security space, entrepreneurs and investors must be able to navigate these challenges and seize these opportunities. This requires a combination of technical expertise, business acumen, and a deep understanding of the blockchain ecosystem and its unique security challenges.

One strategy for success is to focus on developing niche solutions that can address specific security challenges in the blockchain ecosystem. By specializing in a particular area, startups can differentiate themselves from competitors and build a strong reputation as experts in that field.

Another strategy is to partner with established players in the blockchain ecosystem, such as large enterprises or established blockchain companies. This can provide access to resources, expertise, and networks that can help startups to accelerate their growth and gain traction in the market.

Overall, the blockchain security space presents both challenges and opportunities for entrepreneurs and investors. With the right approach and a deep understanding of the ecosystem and its unique security challenges, startups can develop innovative solutions that can help to secure the blockchain and drive further growth and adoption.

## Conclusion
## Key takeaways from the book

Throughout this book, we have explored various aspects of blockchain security, including cross-chain interoperability, zero-knowledge proofs, quantum computing, decentralized governance, and regulatory compliance. In this concluding chapter, we will summarize the key takeaways from each of these topics and discuss their implications for the broader technology landscape.

First and foremost, cross-chain interoperability is critical for the continued growth and adoption of blockchain technology. By enabling different blockchain networks to communicate with each other, cross-chain interoperability can facilitate the development of new applications and use cases for blockchain technology, while also enhancing the security and reliability of the underlying systems.

Second, zero-knowledge proofs are an essential tool for preserving privacy on the blockchain. By enabling parties to prove the validity of a transaction without revealing any sensitive information, zero-knowledge proofs can help to ensure that blockchain-based transactions are both secure and private.

Third, quantum computing poses a significant threat to the security of blockchain systems. While there are currently no practical quantum computing algorithms that can break the underlying cryptographic protocols used in blockchain technology, it is likely only a matter of time before such algorithms are developed. As such, it is essential that blockchain developers and researchers continue to explore and develop quantum-resistant solutions to ensure the long-term security of blockchain systems.

Fourth, decentralized governance is critical for ensuring the security and sustainability of blockchain networks. By distributing decision-making power among network participants, decentralized governance systems can help to prevent any single entity from exerting undue influence over the network, while also ensuring that the network remains responsive to the needs and concerns of its users.

Finally, regulatory compliance is essential for protecting investors and consumers and ensuring the long-term viability of blockchain technology. However, compliance can also present challenges, including increased costs and complexity for blockchain-based businesses. As such, it is essential that regulatory frameworks for blockchain technology strike a balance between protecting consumers and promoting innovation and growth in the industry.

Overall, the key takeaway from this book is that blockchain security is a complex and multifaceted issue that requires a comprehensive and interdisciplinary approach. To ensure the continued growth and adoption of blockchain technology, it is essential that developers, researchers, regulators, and industry stakeholders work together to address the many challenges and opportunities presented by this transformative technology. By doing so, we can unlock the full potential of blockchain technology and create a more secure and equitable digital future for all.

### Implications for the future of blockchain security

As we reach the conclusion of this book on blockchain security, it is clear that the implications for the future of this technology are immense. Blockchain has the potential to revolutionize many industries, from finance to healthcare, but in order for it to reach its full potential, security must be a top priority.

One key implication for the future of blockchain security is the need for continued innovation. As we have seen throughout this book, the security landscape is constantly evolving, and new threats and vulnerabilities are emerging all the time. Therefore, it is essential that the blockchain community continues to invest in research and development to stay ahead of the curve.

Another implication is the need for collaboration and cooperation. Blockchain is a global technology, and it is important that stakeholders work together to develop common standards and best practices for security. This includes not only blockchain developers and researchers, but also regulators, policymakers, and industry associations.

Moreover, as blockchain continues to mature and become more mainstream, we can expect to see greater regulatory scrutiny. This means that compliance will become even more important for blockchain-based businesses, and that they will need to stay up-to-date with evolving regulatory frameworks.

Another implication is the potential for blockchain to be integrated with other emerging technologies, such as artificial intelligence and the Internet of Things. This will create new security challenges, but also new opportunities to enhance security and privacy.

Finally, we must recognize that the security of blockchain is ultimately tied to the security of the broader technology ecosystem. As blockchain becomes more interconnected with other systems and networks, vulnerabilities in those systems can have a cascading effect on the security of blockchain. Therefore, it is important for all stakeholders to prioritize security and work together to address emerging threats.

In conclusion, blockchain is a powerful technology that has the potential to transform many industries, but security must be a top priority if it is to reach its full potential. Continued innovation, collaboration, compliance, and integration with other emerging technologies will be essential for securing the future of blockchain.

## Call to action for stakeholders in the blockchain ecosystem

As the blockchain ecosystem continues to evolve, it is important for all stakeholders to take an active role in ensuring the security and resilience of this technology. This chapter serves as a call to action for stakeholders, including developers, investors, regulators, and users, to work together towards a more secure and trustworthy blockchain ecosystem.

Developers have a crucial role to play in creating secure and resilient blockchain systems. They must prioritize security in the design and development of blockchain applications, ensuring that they follow best practices and are thoroughly tested for vulnerabilities. Additionally, developers should collaborate with security experts to identify potential risks and implement appropriate measures to mitigate them.

Investors also have a responsibility to support blockchain projects that prioritize security and regulatory compliance. They should conduct due diligence before investing in a blockchain project, and be willing to hold project teams accountable for addressing any security concerns that arise.

Regulators also play a key role in ensuring the security and regulatory compliance of blockchain technology. They should work with industry stakeholders to develop clear and consistent regulatory frameworks that protect consumers and investors without stifling innovation. Additionally, regulators should ensure that blockchain projects are held accountable for complying with relevant laws and regulations.

Finally, users of blockchain technology should also take an active role in ensuring its security. They should exercise caution when interacting with blockchain applications, using only trusted and verified platforms. Additionally, they should be willing to report any security concerns they encounter to project teams or regulators.

In conclusion, the future of blockchain security depends on the active participation of all stakeholders. By working together to prioritize security and regulatory compliance, we can create a blockchain ecosystem that is secure, trustworthy, and resilient.

**THE END**

## Key Terms and Definitions

To help you better understand the language and concepts related to aging and older adults, below you will find a list of key terms and their definitions.

1. Blockchain - a decentralized, digital ledger of transactions that is cryptographically secured and maintained by a network of nodes.

2. Consensus algorithm - a method used by blockchain networks to achieve agreement on the state of the ledger. Examples include Proof of Work (PoW), Proof of Stake (PoS), and Delegated Proof of Stake (DPoS).

3. Public key cryptography - a cryptographic system that uses a pair of keys (a public key and a private key) to encrypt and decrypt data. Public key cryptography is used in blockchain networks to ensure secure transactions and access control.

4. Distributed Denial of Service (DDoS) attack - an attack that aims to disrupt the normal functioning of a network or server by overwhelming it with traffic from multiple sources.

5. Smart contract - a self-executing contract with the terms of the agreement between buyer and seller being directly written into lines of code. Smart contracts are used

in blockchain networks to automate the execution of transactions and enforce business logic.

6. Tokenization - the process of representing assets or securities as digital tokens on a blockchain network. Tokenization allows for fractional ownership, increased liquidity, and more efficient trading.

7. Zero-knowledge proof - a cryptographic technique that allows one party to prove knowledge of a secret without revealing the secret itself. Zero-knowledge proofs are used in blockchain networks to ensure privacy and security.

8. Quantum computing - a type of computing that uses quantum bits (qubits) to perform calculations. Quantum computing has the potential to break the cryptographic algorithms used in many blockchain networks.

9. Decentralized Autonomous Organization (DAO) - a decentralized organization that is governed by rules encoded as computer programs on a blockchain network. DAOs allow for decentralized decision-making and management.

10. Regulatory compliance - adherence to the laws, regulations, and guidelines set forth by government agencies and other regulatory bodies. Regulatory compliance is important for blockchain networks to ensure legal compliance and protect investors and consumers.

## Supporting Materials

Introduction:

- Swan, M. (2015). Blockchain: Blueprint for a new economy. O'Reilly Media, Inc.

Chapter 1: Sharding and Scalability:

- Buterin, V. (2018). The scalability trilemma. Ethereum Foundation.
- Zohar, A. (2015). Bitcoin: Under the hood. Communications of the ACM, 58(9), 104-113.
- Popov, S. (2019). The tangle. IOTA Foundation.

Chapter 2: Cross-Chain Interoperability:

- Walch, A., & Clark, D. (2019). Interoperability and the future of blockchain. In J. Bauer & M. Trautwein (Eds.), Handbook of blockchain, digital finance, and inclusion: Cryptocurrency, fintech, insurtech, and regulation (pp. 265-284). Springer International Publishing.
- Coskun, V. (2021). Blockchain Interoperability: Technologies, Challenges, and Future Directions. IEEE Access, 9, 79209-79221.
- Wood, G. (2018). Polkadot: Vision for a heterogeneous multi-chain framework. Parity Technologies.

Chapter 3: Zero-Knowledge Proofs and Privacy:

- Micali, S. (2017). The Algorand platform. Algorand Inc.

- Ben-Sasson, E., Chiesa, A., Tromer, E., & Virza, M. A. (2018). Scalable zero knowledge via cycles of elliptic curves. In Proceedings of the 2018 ACM SIGSAC Conference on Computer and Communications Security (pp. 191-205).
- Zcash. (n.d.). Zcash Protocol Specification.

Chapter 4: Quantum Computing and Blockchain Security:
- Preskill, J. (2018). Quantum computing in the NISQ era and beyond. Quantum, 2, 79.
- Gervais, A., Karame, G. O., Wüst, K., Glykantzis, V., Ritzdorf, H., & Capkun, S. (2016). On the security and performance of proof of work blockchains. In Proceedings of the 2016 ACM SIGSAC Conference on Computer and Communications Security (pp. 3-16).
- Chakraborty, A., Maitra, S., Sanyal, S., & Sen Gupta, S. (2021). A survey of quantum attacks and countermeasures for blockchain and cryptocurrencies. Journal of Network and Computer Applications, 175, 102912.

Chapter 5: Decentralized Governance and Security:
- Kshetri, N., & Voas, J. (2020). Blockchain-enabled decentralized governance: Opportunities and challenges. IT Professional, 22(5), 17-24.
- Teutsch, J., & Reitwiessner, F. (2014). A scalable voting contract. Ethereum Project Yellow Paper, (31).

- Song, J., Kim, Y., Kim, T., & Han, J. (2021). Review and future research directions on blockchain governance. Journal of Information Security and Applications, 59, 102858.

Chapter 6: Regulatory Compliance and Security:

- Financial Action Task Force. (2019). Guidance for a risk-based approach to virtual assets and virtual asset service providers.

- Grinberg, R. (2018). Bitcoin: An innovative alternative digital currency. Hastings Science & Technology Law Journal, 10(1), 1-64.

Conclusion

Antonopoulos, A. M. (2014). Mastering Bitcoin: Unlocking Digital Cryptocurrencies. O'Reilly Media, Inc.

Böhme, R., Christin, N., Edelman, B., & Moore, T. (2015). Bitcoin: economics, technology, and governance. Journal of Economic Perspectives, 29(2), 213-238.

Crosby, M., Pattanayak, P., Verma, S., & Kalyanaraman, V. (2016). Blockchain technology: beyond bitcoin. Applied Innovation, 2(6-10), 71-81.

DuPont, Q. (2018). The crypto-anarchist manifesto. In Bitcoin and Beyond (pp. 3-15). Routledge.

Ethereum Foundation. (2021). Ethereum: A Next-Generation Smart Contract and Decentralized Application Platform. Retrieved from https://ethereum.org/en/

Grigg, I. (2019). The Ricardian Contract. Retrieved from https://iang.org/papers/ricardian_contract.html

Nakamoto, S. (2008). Bitcoin: A Peer-to-Peer Electronic Cash System. Retrieved from https://bitcoin.org/bitcoin.pdf

Swan, M. (2015). Blockchain: blueprint for a new economy. O'Reilly Media, Inc.

Wattenhofer, R. (2016). The science of blockchain. In Advances in Cryptology–CRYPTO 2016 (pp. 3-4). Springer.

www.ingramcontent.com/pod-product-compliance
Lightning Source LLC
LaVergne TN
LVHW010410070526
838199LV00065B/5929